I0844828

Entrepreneurial Enlightenment

Buddha's Wisdom for Business

Table of Contents

Chapter 1. Introduction

Discover a revolutionary way to navigate the challenging world of business in our Special Report, "Entrepreneurial Enlightenment: Buddha's Wisdom for Business." This unique guide melds ancient wisdom with modern entrepreneurship, ensuring you walk the path of success with grace, empathy, and inner peace. Prepare to read about business strategies illuminated by Buddha's teachings, unlocking success secrets rooted in mindfulness, resilience, and balance. Perfect for forward-thinking individuals, this report is anything but ordinary business literature—it's a journey of self-discovery, blending spirituality and business acumen to create holistic success. Let's explore entrepreneurship through a refreshingly tranquil lens. Are you ready to be thoroughly enlightened? Your path to entrepreneurial nirvana awaits!

Chapter 2. Understanding Buddha's Teachings: A Preliminary Insight

The teachings of Buddha, known as Dhamma, reveal profound insights about life and the nature of existence. Diving into these teachings and integrating them into your business practices will offer a profound shift in perspective that can encourage innovation, improve decision-making, and foster a harmonious organizational climate.

2.1. The Four Noble Truths

The foundation of Buddha's teachings lies in the Four Noble Truths, which encapsulate the core of Buddhist philosophy.

1. Dukkha (Suffering): Life in the material and corporate world is intrinsically filled with dissatisfaction, stress, and suffering.

2. Samudaya (Origin of Suffering): This suffering arises from our desires, cravings, and clinging, analogous to the way a business may hold onto outdated practices or obsess over profits.

3. Nirodha (Cessation of Suffering): The cessation of this suffering can be achieved by letting go of these desires and cravings, much as an entrepreneur learns to let go of strict control and gives their team room to grow.

4. Magga (Path to Cessation of Suffering): The path to cessation of suffering is embodied in the Eightfold Path.

The acknowledgement of suffering and its origins allows us to comprehend the challenge, which in business translates to identifying obstacles. The belief in a path towards the cessation of suffering endorses the belief in solutions.

2.2. The Eightfold Path

The Eightfold Path provides a practical guideline for personal improvement, and can also serve as a roadmap for effective business management and leadership.

1. Right Understanding: Understanding the realities of business, its objectives, competition, and market dynamics is fundamental to success.

2. Right Thought: This encourages benevolence and empathy, crucial for maintaining positive employee relations and customer support.

3. Right Speech: Clear, truthful, and helpful communication strengthens team cooperation and enhances customer trust.

4. Right Action: Ethical conduct respects all stakeholders, enhancing the brand image and reputation.

5. Right Livelihood: Choosing industries and occupations that do no harm means growth is aligned with societal health.

6. Right Effort: Persistence and dedication ensure that goals are met despite challenges.

7. Right Mindfulness: Awareness of the current situation promotes agile decision-making and snaps the trap of complacency.

8. Right Concentration: Unwavering focus on strategic goals provides a clear vision for everyone involved in the business.

2.3. Mindfulness in Business

Mindfulness, a critical aspect of Buddha's teachings, goes a long way in modern business. Often, business leaders are so engrossed in future projections and past performances that they lose touch with the present. This lessens the ability to make sound decisions; a mindful leader, however, stays present, alert, and open to new possibilities, enabling more flexible and creative solutions.

2.4. Karma in Business

Karma is a natural law in Buddhism, simply stated as, "what goes around comes around." In business, every action taken, including product quality, customer service, employee treatment, and business ethics, directly or indirectly leads to results that impact the company. Understanding karma can prompt businesses to act responsibly.

2.5. Embracing Impermanence

In Buddhism, life is viewed as a constant state of flux and change. This corresponds to the ever-changing nature of businesses in response to market trends, technologies, and consumer preferences. Acceptance of impermanence leads to resilience during times of change and upheaval.

2.6. The Middle Way in Business

The Middle Way in Buddhism is a path of moderation, avoiding extremes of indulgence or asceticism. Applied in business, it suggests a balance between profit generation and social responsibility, growth and sustainability, competition and cooperation.

Understanding and applying Buddha's teachings can revolutionize the way you perceive and handle your business. They cultivate a kinder and more mindful leadership style, promote ethical business practices, and encourage a thriving work environment that aligns profitability with purpose. This entrepreneurial enlightenment could arguably be a path to not just financial success, but holistic success and inner peace in the demanding, challenging world of business.

Embodying these insights invites entrepreneurs to challenge the conventional, enabling them to explore business with not just a desire to succeed, but with the intention of enlightenment, serving as a beacon of positivity in the corporate world.

Chapter 3. From Mindfulness to Market: Applying Buddhist Principles to Business Models

Buddhism and business may seem worlds apart, but the synergies between both are potent, waiting to be harnessed. From its origin, Buddhism focuses on understanding ourselves and connecting harmoniously with the world surrounding us. It's a path rooted in maintaining balance, fostering mindfulness, and cultivating resilience—traits strikingly relevant and desperately needed in the world of business.

3.1. Ushering Mindfulness into the Boardroom

Modern business demands quick decisions, swift action, and prompt results. Entrepreneurship, particularly, is a constant race against time, leaving little room for pause. Amid this swirl of activity, the importance of being present in the current moment gets lost— a principle that Buddhism deeply emphasizes.

Incorporating mindfulness into one's daily business practice, therefore, serves multiple purposes. Firstly, it allows you to be acutely aware of your thoughts, actions, and their consequences. It helps you to pivot away from autopilot mode, bringing purpose, care, and attention to your tasks, however trivial they might be. This heightened awareness and presence of mind intensify focus, amplifying productivity.

Moreover, a mindful entrepreneur is more in tune with their emotions, maintaining composure even under stress. By promoting clarity of thought, mindfulness also nourishes better decision making, an aspect pivotal to business success.

3.2. Resilience: The Core of Entrepreneurial Success

Entrepreneurship is a path fraught with challenges. In the face of adversities, resilience serves as the antidote, helping entrepreneurs to weather the storm and bounce back stronger. It's the ability to react positively even to failure, treating every setback as a stepping stone to move forward.

Buddhism cultivates resilience by promoting the acceptance of impermanence and encouraging us to respond instead of react. The practice of meditation— a cornerstone of Buddhist principles— fosters mental resilience, enhancing our ability to adapt and persevere through challenges.

3.3. Balancing Profit and Purpose

While profitability is a measure of business success, Buddhism instructs us to delve deeper into the essence of our actions—our intent. The principle here is the "Middle Way," which in a business context means balancing the pursuit of profit with a larger purpose that benefits society.

Buddhist-inspired businesses learn to marry their profit motives with a central guiding purpose that uplifts, energizes, and inspires their work. This balance ensures that while the organization as a whole follows a path of profitability, they equally contribute to societal well-being.

3.4. Engaging Ethically

The incorporation of the fundamental Buddhist precepts into

business activities anchors operations in morality and ethics. These precepts prohibit actions that harm others—killing, stealing, dishonesty, sexual misconduct, and intoxication. In business terms, it involves embracing fair trade practices, ensuring a safe working environment, and promoting honesty and integrity.

The Buddhist principle of Right Livelihood is especially relevant here. It encourages entrepreneurs to engage in business activities that spread positivity and do no harm. This principle runs counter to the sometimes cut-throat world of business, providing a sustainable and ethical approach to commerce.

3.5. Leading with Compassion

The profound philosophy of compassion that Buddhism espouses holds considerable value for today's business leaders. Compassionate leaders prioritize the welfare of their employees and stakeholders. They foster a culture that supports mental well-being, encourages open communication, and nurtures a sense of belonging. This approach invariably leads to increased employee satisfaction, higher retention rates, and a more harmonious organizational environment, directly influencing business success.

In conclusion, the Buddhist principles of mindfulness, resilience, ethical engagement, balance, and compassion create a sustainable framework for entrepreneurial success. When adopted wholeheartedly, they do not just contribute to business prosperity, but also develop a spiritually enlightened entrepreneur, creating an atmosphere of positivity, peace, and success. The potential of this holistic success model is limitless and lies waiting to be harnessed in the realm of modern business.

Chapter 4. Enlightened Leadership: Incorporating Compassion and Wisdom in Decision Making

Entrepreneurship requires making decisions, often under high pressure and with restricted resources. To excel in this demanding environment, an enlightened leader embraces the wisdom and compassion of Buddha's teachings. Rooted in mindfulness, resilience, and balance, these principles offer a holistic approach to leadership and entrepreneurial success.

4.1. Mindfulness in Leadership

Mindfulness is a process that enables us to be fully present and attentive to our actions, thoughts, and feelings. It's not about stopping or controlling the thoughts but allowing them to flow freely without judgment. It's about observing rather than interpreting or reacting to them.

Applied to leadership, mindfulness allows leaders to remain more calm and focused, even in the midst of chaos. It also sharpens their ability to discern patterns, connect the dots, and make strategic decisions. By being fully present, they can communicate more effectively, feel deeply connected to their team, and lead with more authenticity and empathy.

Incorporating mindfulness into decision-making can be done by:

1. Practicing meditation: Regular meditation calms the mind, allowing clearer thoughts, enhanced creativity, improved concentration, and better decision-making. It also helps manage

stress effectively.

2. Maintaining mind-body harmony: Regular exercise, balanced nutrition, adequate sleep, and staying hydrated all contribute to maintaining a sound mind, leading to wise decisions.

4.2. Compassion in Leadership

Buddha taught that compassion, the desire to alleviate suffering, is core to being enlightened. Compassion-driven leadership fuels higher levels of collaboration and makes a team more resilient during challenging times. It creates an environment where everyone feels they matter, leading to increased loyalty, productivity, and innovation.

To incorporate compassion into decision-making:

1. Be empathetic: Understand the perspectives and experiences of others. An empathetic leader is a good listener, good observer, and good communicator.

2. Practice kindness: Kindness should not be mistaken for weakness. It can be as simple as recognizing the efforts and accomplishments of others, lending a hand when needed, or speaking respectfully.

3. Promote inclusivity: Encourage an atmosphere in which everyone feels valued and heard. In a diverse team, giving everyone an equal opportunity to express their thoughts can lead to better decisions.

4.3. Wisdom in Leadership

The capacity to make sound judgments and make the right decisions is essential for enlightened leadership. Wisdom, according to Buddha, comes from self-knowledge, experience, and continual learning.

Incorporating wisdom into decision-making:

1. Embrace the clarity of thought: Leaders who are mindful can choose the right path with clarity and conviction. They understand when to act and when to remain patient, when to jump on an opportunity, and when to let it go.

2. Learn from experience: Every event or situation is a potential learning opportunity. A wise leader sees value in failures and treats them as stepping stones to success.

3. Practice reflection: Regular self-reflection allows leaders to learn about themselves, their actions, and decisions, promoting growth and transformation.

4.4. Balance in Leadership

Balance may well be the most challenging aspect of enlightened leadership. It's about making the hard decisions while nurturing the soft human souls charged to your leadership. A balanced leader knows when to show strength and when to exhibit grace.

To incorporate balance into decision-making:

1. Balance logic and emotion: Emotions are important, but they should not solely dictate decisions. Weigh the pros and cons, and consider the emotional ramifications of choices before making a decision.

2. Balance risk and caution: It is crucial for leaders to take risks to grow, but they should also calculate and manage those risks carefully.

3. Balance profit and purpose: A business needs to generate profit, but it should also contribute value to the community.

Enlightened leadership is a journey, not a destination. With mindfulness and compassion in our hearts, wisdom in our minds, and balance in our decisions, we can navigate the challenging landscapes of entrepreneurship and hence, achieve holistic success. These principles, when lived daily, can transform the way we perceive leadership and impact the success of our endeavors.

Chapter 5. Embracing Impermanence: A Fresh Perspective on Business Sustainability

In a world of constant change, the always-relatable teachings of Buddha succinctly preach the impermanence of everything. This very concept, if applied correctly, offers a fresh outlook on business sustainability. The process of constant change is eternally underway, and being in-tune with it is a recipe for remarkable resilience and long-term success.

5.1. Embracing Change, Embracing Growth

Understanding the impermanent nature of business is the key first step. Whether we talk about consumer trends, competition, technology, or even the dynamics of a team—and especially in light of recent global events—change is an inherent aspect of the business landscape. Like the ebb and flow of the sea, the business world moves rhythmically yet inconsistently.

Buddha asserted that everything in existence is transient, ever-changing. When we apply this wisdom to businesses, it gives us a gentle yet transformative reminder: if we are not growing or evolving, we are likely moving backwards. Hence, successful entrepreneurs are those capable of embracing this change, adapting, and growing with it.

Reactive approach to change, although useful at times, generally puts one on the back foot, being always a responder and not the originator. A more strategic approach is one that anticipates change and prepares for it. Investing in research and being abreast with technological advancements, societal changes, and market trends is pivotal, as is being prepared to steer the business in the corresponding direction.

5.2. The Impermanence of Success and Failure

Another insightful interpretation of Buddha's wisdom is how it applies to the achievements and hardships we encounter. Just as everything else, moments of triumph and defeat are inconstant. They, too, are fleeting, and will inevitably pass.

Instead of resting on laurels of past victories, we should perceive success as an encouragement to keep moving forward, taking preventive measures to stave off complacency. Celebrating your victories is important, but even more so is comprehending that they are transient.

Similarly, failure is not permanent. Every setback is brimming with potential learning experiences. In the throes of a failing enterprise, remaining aware that failure is not permanent can help regain perspective, directing energy towards harvesting lessons and making strategic adjustments.

5.3. Transformational Leadership: The Impermanence of Self

Impermanence also extends to our individual roles and identities within a business. The traditional view of a stable, unchanging leadership is not realistic in the modern world. The role of an entrepreneur in the early stages of a startup is drastically different from their role when the company becomes a mature business.

Transformational leadership takes center stage here, advocating for flexibility and continual personal growth as vital components of sustainability. Leaders, like businesses, need to adapt and grow with the changing demands of their roles. An entrepreneurial leader needs to view their identity as impermanent, fluid, and ripe for constant improvement.

Entrepreneurs who are able to expand and shift their skills and mindset with the changing needs of their business position themselves, and their ventures, far stronger for long-term sustainability.

5.4. Lessons from Nature: Sustainable Strategies

Nature, the embodiment of impermanence, provides potent insights for sustainable business strategies. No season lasts forever; everything has its moment, then paves the way for something new. This cyclical nature throws light on the impermanence of trends, products, and services in the business realm.

Striving for ever-green business operations should be replaced with the acknowledgement that certain elements have a limited lifespan. Businesses must be prepared to develop, adapt, phase out, and phase in products and services as per market demands. The key is to recognize that nothing lasts forever and being prepared to evolve and, if needed, let go, is the path to long-term operational sustainability.

5.5. Business Models and Buddha: Impermanence as a Guiding Principle

Incorporating the understanding of impermanence in a business model can revolutionize strategy formulation and execution. Traditional rigid business plans are being replaced with flexible, evolving models that change with the dynamics of the market.

By expecting change, predicting it, and gearing for it, businesses can create a cycle of continuous improvement, where impermanence becomes a driving force rather than a disruptor. This makes organizations resilient and adaptive, qualities that are indispensable in the fluid and fast-paced business environment.

Buddha's wise teachings tell us that accepting and understanding the impermanent nature of life can guide us towards peace. In the context of business, understanding and leveraging impermanence equip entrepreneurs to navigate change, leading to sustainable growth and enlightened entrepreneurship.

Your business need not be a static entity in an ever-changing world. Embrace impermanence, adapt gracefully, grow intelligently and create a successful, sustainable venture that thrives amidst chaos and change. The path to achieving this may not always be as tranquil as a Buddhist monastery, but it can at least be filled with gentle wisdom. A business that can tap into this powerful truth of existence is a business braced for true long-term success.

Chapter 6. Bhavana in Business: Cultivating Mindfulness for Enhanced Productivity

In this rapidly changing business world, rattling at breakneck speed, silence and stillness might seem out of place or even counterproductive. However, it's this exact silence, the tranquility offered by mindfulness, which forms our discussion's core. The concept we delve into owes its lineage to the Buddha: Bhāvanā, translated best to 'cultivation,' with a special focus on cultivating mindfulness for enhanced productivity within business settings.

6.1. Mindfulness in Business

Mindfulness, in its fundamental form, refers to the finely tuned awareness of the present moment. It's about experiencing the right now, in its raw, unadulterated form, free from preconceived notions or judgments. In our quest for achievements and results, we often fall into the trap of constantly chasing future goals, forgetting to live and breathe in the 'now.' This disconnection can trigger stress, burnout, or a lack of fulfillment, crippling not just individuals but also businesses.

Incorporating mindfulness into one's professional life can lead to enhanced focus, better decision-making, improved problem-solving skills, and relationships. It creates a resilient workforce capable of dealing with turbulent times without losing its balance.

Now, you might be wondering about the journey from being aware of mindfulness to embedding it in business. This transition is termed Bhāvanā, or cultivation. Let's now explore the threefold path to cultivating mindfulness akin to agriculture: Prepare the land, plant the seeds, and nurture them to sprout.

6.2. Bhāvanā: Preparing the Mind 'Land'

The first step to Bhāvanā is preparing the mind, akin to how a farmer prepares his land for cultivation. It involves creating fertile mental ground conducive to mindfulness. This preparation is twofold: mental decluttering and mental nurturing.

Mental Decluttering involves removing negative emotions such as fear, anger, anxiety, or any other mental debris that could hinder the growth of mindfulness. It's about creating space in your mind by letting go of distractive thoughts and harmful attitudes.

Mental Nurturing, on the other hand, is about cultivating positive mental attitudes of kindness, compassion, and empathy. These attitudes help to foster an environment that encourages and supports mindfulness.

6.3. Planting the Mindfulness 'Seeds'

Having prepared the mind 'land', the next step is to plant the seeds—introducing mindfulness practices in your daily routine.

One of the easiest ways to begin is by practicing mindful breathing. It's a simple exercise where you focus on your breath going in and out. This practice may seem simple, but it helps you anchor your mind to the present, paving the way for greater awareness that can be leveraged in decision-making and creative thinking in business.

There are other ways to foster mindfulness too: mindfully eating your lunch, fully focussed and aware of the tastes and textures; taking 'awareness' walks where you dwell on the environment around - the sound, sights, and smell; or even practicing mindful listening during meetings.

6.4. Nurturing the Mindfulness 'Plants'

Once you've sown the seeds of mindfulness, the third and arguably, the most crucial step of Bhāvanā, is nurturing these tiny plants into resilient trees. It's achieved by setting an intention to be mindful and making a concerted effort towards it each day.

Daily practice is crucial to this nurturing process. Just as regular watering helps a plant grow, daily mindfulness practices help strengthen and deepen your ability to stay present. With practice, mindfulness gradually stops being an 'activity' and turns into an 'attitude,' naturally ingrained in your thought process and actions.

Another vital element to nurturing is patience. It's important not to rush the process or get disheartened if results aren't immediate. Like any significant change, mindfulness too takes time to permeate into all corners of your life and manifest its benefits.

6.5. Reaping the Business 'Harvest'

So, what does one gain with mindfulness? Personal benefits aside, businesses stand to reap numerous benefits from cultivating mindfulness.

One of the immediate advantages is increased productivity. Studies have shown that mindfulness aids in reducing distractions and improving focus, consequently enhancing work efficiency.

Moreover, it promotes empathy and compassion. In a business environment, it can translate into better people management, improved relationships, better client interactions, and a more harmonious work environment, all of which contribute to long-term business success.

Lastly, cultivating mindfulness helps in building emotional resilience, acting as a shock absorber in challenging situations. It enables one to deal with stress and setbacks with grace, making it an essential trait for leaders.

In conclusion, this journey of Bhāvanā—cultivating mindfulness in business—is not a quick-fix solution to business problems. Instead, it is a gradual internal transformation bringing about a change from a state of 'Doing' to one of 'Being'. It's about fostering an approach that blends professional prowess with personal fulfillment for an all-round successful entrepreneurial journey. As Buddha rightly said, "The mind is everything. What you think, you become." So, make your mind your friend, cultivate mindfulness, and harness its power to create successful, empathic, and resilient businesses.

Chapter 7. Single-Pointed Concentration: Leveraging Business Focus

The journey of an entrepreneur is often centered around multitasking. From managing employees and developing business strategies to pitching ideas to investors, the entrepreneurial road is multifaceted and demands unwavering focus. It echoes Buddha's teachings on single-pointed concentration—dedicating focus entirely to one task at a time as a way of fostering a sharper, more focused mind— a crucial overlooked asset that promises to catapult your business success.

7.1. The Essence of Single-Pointed Concentration

Single-pointed concentration, or Samadhi, is a mental discipline taught by Buddha nearly 2500 years ago. It's about maintaining unwavering focus on a single point or task. It's about the ability to keep the mind from straying into past or future thoughts, but instead, fully immerse in the present moment. For entrepreneurs, incorporating Samadhi into your daily work tasks can aid better decision making, foster creativity, and enhance overall business performance.

Meditation is key to cultivating single-pointed concentration. It serves to direct your focus towards your breathing, a mantra, or a specific mental image. The objective, however, is not just about achieving a heightened focus. It's about understanding the fluctuations of your mind and recognizing that you have the ability to control where your focus goes.

7.2. Applying Single-Pointed Concentration in Business

As an entrepreneur, you're no stranger to a convoluted workday entrenched in a myriad of tasks. It's easy to fall into the survival mode of 'doing more in less time.' However, single-pointed concentration calls for an alternative approach. It insists on dedicating complete attention to a solitary task before moving onto the next.

Mastering single-pointed concentration can reduce the impact of distractions and elevate efficiency. Your mind begins to function optimally, providing clearer insights, sharper creativity, and superior problem-solving skills. In a business context, this effectiveness can translate into improved product development, better management strategies, and a cleaner vision for the future.

Using mindfulness meditation as a tool, start by setting aside a specific time in the day to immerse yourself completely in single tasks. Incrementally increase this period as your ability to focus enhances. Remember, it's not about accomplishing multiple tasks concurrently, but about the profound understanding and accomplishment of each individual task.

7.3. Inspiring Employee Concentration

Cultivating a sense of single-pointed concentration amongst your employees can create a harmonious and focused work environment. When the entire team is aligned in concentration, the output is bound to witness a significant uptick.

Start by offering mindfulness training to every team member, carving out time in the day for them to engage in concentrated, uninterrupted work. Encouraging regular breaks and incorporating a culture of mindful meetings where multitasking is discouraged can also build a more focused, productive workforce.

7.4. Sustainable Success through Concentration

The outcome of implementing single-pointed concentration in your business is sustainable success. A clear, focused mind can lead to better business decisions, fostering a company that's not just reactive but proactive too. Moreover, it allows you to bring about a balance between work and personal life. By completely immersing yourself into the task at hand, whether it's a business meeting or spending time with family, brings about higher satisfaction levels.

Single-pointed concentration is an age-old practice that can bring about drastic, positive changes in the modern business world. By incorporating this into your entrepreneurial journey, you can lay down a foundation for a focused, efficient, balanced and successful future in business.

Chapter 8. The Power of Altruism: Reimagining Competitive Advantage

In a cutthroat business landscape, the traditional model of leveraging competitive advantage often emphasizes winner-takes-all strategies. While these tactics may yield short-term gains, they risk undermining the long-term success, sustainability, and harmony of the ventures in question. What if we consider reenvisioning competitive advantage not as a zero-sum game but rather, through the lens of altruism, as a win-win situation?

8.1. Altruism Defined: A Fundamental Paradigm Shift

Altruism is a concept deeply ingrained in the teachings of Buddha, where emphasis is placed on selfless concern for the well-being of others. It calls for actions that are not selfishly motivated but instead prioritize the welfare of others. It is an outward-focused approach, a call to see and engage with the world mindfully and compassionously.

In the context of business, such a model may seem counterintuitive. Many may argue, "Does not business, by its very nature, entail profit-making and self-interest?" Herein lies the fundamental paradigm shift—business, like any human endeavor, is capable of evolving. And it is upon this transformative path that a bridge between business and altruism can be built, an approach to entrepreneurship that merges profit with empathy, competition with compassion.

8.2. The Altruistic Advantage: From Transactions to Relationships

The key to integrating altruism into business practice lies in shifting the focus from transactions to relationships. A business enterprise should not view its customers merely as sources of revenue but as valued stakeholders who deserve respect, honesty, and quality service. This outlook engenders increased trust, loyalty, and satisfaction among customers, building patronage and enhancing market standing in the process.

Simultaneously, an altruistic approach motivates the business to consider the welfare of its employees and shareholders, recognizing their contributions and striving for their well-being. It encourages the establishment of fair policies, the provision of adequate benefits, and the creation of a healthy and nurturing work environment. Such practices go far beyond financial metrics of success, fostering an organizational culture that values people, and thereby cultivates commitment, productivity, and perseverance.

8.3. Redefining Competition: Towards Cooperative Success

By infusing the philosophy of altruism into your business model, it no longer becomes about beating the opponent. Instead, it inspires a perspective that views competitors as potential collaborators. An altruistic approach in business ventures can potentially take several forms: forging partnerships to achieve mutual goals, sharing resources to minimize waste, or cross-promoting each other's products and services where synergies exist. This synergistic mindset, while elevating your business, contributes to the collective growth of the industrial ecosystem.

8.4. Altruism and Innovation: Towards Sustainable Business Practices

Altruism also serves as a catalyst for innovation aimed at sustainability. Businesses grounded in the principles of altruism get motivated to develop products and services beneficial to society and the environment. By adopting eco-friendly practices or investing in renewable energy, for example, businesses not only satisfy their entrepreneurial journey but also contribute to the well-being of our planet.

This kind of value creation necessitates a heightened level of consciousness—a mindfulness that goes beyond revenue to consider the larger picture of societal and environmental impacts. It requires the wisdom to understand that a business's profitability and societal prosperity are not dichotomous but intertwined aspects of sustainability.

8.5. Entrepreneurial Enlightenment: Buddha's Wisdom in Modern Business

Infusing the practice of altruism in entrepreneurship calls for a profound shift—one that assures success not at the cost of others but as a culmination of shared value creation. Buddha's teachings on selfless service and empathy serve to reframe competition as opportunities for mutual growth, encouraging a balance between profit-making and societal progress.

The principles of altruism and mindfulness—as taught by Buddha—urge an entrepreneurial journey nestled in shared prosperity, mindful action, and peaceful coexistence. Businesses are then no longer seen as mere financial entities but as platforms for positive societal change, fostering an entrepreneurial landscape adorned with empathy, compassion, collaboration, and sustainable growth.

Indeed, this is the business model of the future—a model nurtured by the power of altruism. By reimagining competitive advantage through these lenses, we unlock a new realm of entrepreneurial enlightenment, a business space imbued with holistic success. Only by forging this mindful path can we ensure that our entrepreneurial endeavors contribute to, rather than detract from, the creation of a more compassionate and equitable world.

Chapter 9. Business Karma: Ethical Practices for Sustainable Growth

The concept of Karma, derived from ancient Buddhist teachings, refers to the belief that consequences are the direct result of individual actions. When applied to the realm of business, this principle becomes a tool for shaping strategies and making decisions that ensure sustainable growth. By practicing ethical enterprise — benefiting customers, the environment, and society at large — we position ourselves to receive favorable results in turn. As the saying goes, "You reap what you sow."

9.1. From Buddha's Lips to the Boardroom

The core teachings of Buddha carry a timeless wisdom, perfectly applicable to the cutthroat dynamics of the business world. The philosophy of interconnectedness is pivotal here — in recognizing that we are all interdependent, we should strive for the upliftment of others. This perspective enables us to avoid engaging in harmful practices that might yield temporary gains, but adversely affect our long-term business trajectory and relationships.

An action, or Karma, is deemed ethical if it results in happiness and positivity for others without causing harm or disruptions. Therefore, the Karma principle underscores the importance of ethical practices in business. Here are some ways to integrate business karma in the everyday:

1. Strive to be fair and honest in all dealings.

2. Respect the rights and interests of stakeholders.

3. Nurture a considerate and inclusive workplace culture.

4. Prioritize customer satisfaction and forge lasting relationships.

5. Engage in socially responsible initiatives.

9.2. The Ethical Practices Framework

It's one thing to grasp the concept of business karma; it's another to implement it effectively. Here is a succinct Ethical Practices Framework that can aid your journey towards ethical entrepreneurship:

Record and Implement Ethical Standards

Establishing clear, enforceable ethical standards is the first step towards fostering a culture of ethical business practices. These parameters should be well-documented and disseminated among all members of your business—from top leadership to new hires—ensuring everyone is aware of the expectations.

Transparent Operations

Transparency boosts trust among customers, employees, and stakeholders. Maintaining open channels of communication can ward off suspicions and disgruntlement. Keep all parties informed about decisive factors, be it operational changes, financial statuses, or strategic approaches.

Ethical Training and Educational Programs

Introducing regular training and educational programs can ensure that ethical standards are understood and adhered to. These initiatives should foster shared responsibility and accountability among your staff. Additionally, they provide opportunities for open discussions on ethical dilemmas and potential solutions.

Fostering a Culture of Accountability

Accountability is integral to maintaining ethical standards. A robust structure of checks and balances can ensure every party is held accountable for their actions. Encourage employees to report any unethical conduct without the fear of retaliation.

Corporate Social Responsibility (CSR)

Corporate social responsibility is the embodiment of business karma. Implementing CSR initiatives showcases a business that is not solely about amassing profits but is also committed to the betterment of society and the environment.

=== A Balanced Scale: Profits and Purpose

Moving forward ethically doesn't mean sacrificing profitability. In fact, there's an increasing body of evidence suggesting that businesses practicing high ethical standards yield higher profits in the long-term. A reputation for integrity and transparency can attract loyal customers and dedicated employees.

Moreover, by contributing to societal welfare, companies indirectly foster an environment where their ventures can thrive. Companies that invest in improving societal conditions, environmental conservation, and employee welfare find that the benefits—though not instantly quantifiable—have a significant long-term impact.

A balanced scale of profit and purpose results in harmonious growth — a virtuous cycle of giving and receiving that reinforces itself. This is the essence of business karma — the noble path to sustainable and equitable growth.

=== Walking the Talk: Case Studies

To illustrate the principles discussed, let's explore a few case studies of companies that have successfully implemented business karma.

Patagonia

Outdoor clothing company Patagonia's commitment to corporate responsibility is an integral part of its business model. They invest in environmental conservation, use recycled or organically produced materials, and value fair labor practices. This has earned them a devoted customer base and a reputation for ethics and sustainability.

The Body Shop

Known for its anti-animal testing stance since its inception, The Body Shop practices ethical sourcing and fair-trade. These commendable practices have not hindered their growth, but instead have contributed to their brand's strength and customer loyalty.

Everlane

This clothing company is distinguished by its extreme transparency. Everlane shares in-depth information about product raw material sourcing, factory conditions, and pricing. This ethical practice ensures loyal customers and draws the attention of those seeking ethically sourced products.

These companies exemplify integrating business karma and corporate responsibility into their ethos. This approach has not only ensured a sustainable growth trajectory but also garnered customer loyalty, workforce dedication, and overall societal approval.

In conclusion, adopting ethical practices aligns with the karma principle, guiding businesses towards sustainable growth. A reciprocal relationship of respect, fairness, and beneficence between a business and its environment results in mutual advancement—providing a true illustration of business karma in action. By observing such practices, you sow the seeds for a prosperous future, fostering an enterprise that thrives in harmony with society and the planet. After all, in the world of business, like in life, what goes around, indeed comes around.

== The Middle Path: Balancing Profit and Purpose
In the swirl of entrepreneurship, achieving balance tends to take a backseat. Obsessed with productivity and profits, we are prone to lose sight of purpose, creating an imbalance that is a breeding ground for stress, burnout, and a severe lack of fulfillment. The solution, as we will see, can be found in embracing a concept intrinsic to the Buddha's teachings: The Middle Path also known as The Eightfold Path, a doctrine advocating for

moderation and balance in all aspects of life.

=== The Middle Ground in Business

Delving into the Buddha's teachings, the 'Middle Path' stands as a principal concept proposing the adoption of moderation in our lives. Often, we rue the existence of polar opposites: success and failure, delight and despair, profit and loss. The Buddha taught that true wisdom lies in understanding the interdependence of these polarities and maintaining a balanced stance.

From a business viewpoint, the Middle Path emphasizes

meeting points between opposing entities. It rallies for a fair distribution of profit, stakeholder value, and social purpose. To reach this equilibrium, entrepreneurs must understand that their ventures serve two masters: Profit and Purpose. Profit enables the business's survival, while Purpose gives it meaning.

Blind pursuit of profit can lead to unethical choices, environmental damage, and simmering discontent among stakeholders. On the other hand, solely focusing on a purpose means running the risk of poor financial performance, making it challenging to sustain the business.

The Middle Path's crux is realizing that neither extreme is viable. Striking a balance between profit and purpose ensures not just the firm's sustainability, but also ignites passion and engagement among its employees, projecting a promising image to the clients and wider society.

=== Translating Wisdom to Practice

To walk the Middle Path in a business context, understanding and practicing the Eightfold Path elements can provide an invaluable road map. These eight areas of practice—right understanding, right intention, right speech, right action, right livelihood, right effort, right mindfulness, and right concentration—when interpreted from a business perspective, can create a synergy of profit and purpose.

'Right Understanding' involves a thorough comprehension of your business model, it's impact on the society and environment, and grasping the concept of impermanence, that businesses must adapt to the ever-changing market dynamics to thrive.

'Right Intention' means leading your business based on positive and ethical motives. A business should not merely be a tool for amassing wealth, but a platform for creating value—for the customers, employees, and society as a whole.

'Right Speech' refers to honest, transparent, and open communication with your stakeholders. It also means using your business as a platform to send out positive messages, create awareness, or advocate social issues.

'Right Action' signifies conducting

business fairly and ethically. In an era where corporate malfeasance can lead to disastrous outcomes, this is a non-negotiable factor for any venture intending to walk the Middle Path.

'Right Livelihood' suggests that the business in itself should serve some positive purpose and not harm others. This involves offering valuable products or services that improve life quality or solve pressing problems, adhering to fair labor practices, and minimizing environmental impact.

'Right Effort' underscores the importance of continuous improvement, resilience, and persistence. It involves cultivating good habits, improving processes, products and services, and maintaining a continuous learning culture within the team.

'Right Mindfulness' means being fully aware and attentive to the present situation of the business. Monitoring your business environment, including social, technological, and market trends, will enable the entrepreneur to make informed, agile decisions.

'Right Concentration' involves the necessity for businesses to focus on their core competencies while maintaining strategic flexibility. It is about mindful prioritization, sticking to what the business knows best, and not losing sight of the larger purpose amidst the buzz of everyday operations.

=== Maintaining Balance: A Case for Mindfulness in Business

Mindfulness, at its core, is about achieving a state of active, open attention to the present. This wisdom holds significant implications for modern entrepreneurship. When we are mindful, we observe our thoughts and feelings from a distance, without judging them as good or bad. This state of presence helps us respond to business situations with calmness, clarity, and compassion.

Applying mindfulness in business situations allows us to be more aware of our internal states, the environment around us, and how we're relating to others. It helps us be intentional about where we devote our energies, aligning our actions with our overall business purpose.

Moreover, a mindful approach fosters empathy, enabling leaders to resonate more effectively with their team members and clients, solidifying relationships and creating a nurturing work environment. This not only attracts and retains top talent but also results in more satisfied, loyal customers, driving business growth and profitability.

=== Navigating Challenges and Impermanence in Business

The Middle Path does not assure absence of challenges. In fact, Buddhism considers suffering as an inevitable part of life. However, it provides tools to manage such suffering. One such powerful concept is the realization of impermanence.

Applying the

principle of impermanence in business can be immensely liberating. Businesses operate in dynamic, ever-evolving environments. Market trends fluctuate, consumer preferences shift, competition intensifies, and crises occur. By acknowledging this constant state of change, entrepreneurs can equip themselves to be more adaptable and agile, responding promptly and efficiently to the changing landscape.

Innovation and continuous learning become essential tools in navigating this impermanence. An entrepreneurial venture that adheres to the Middle Path is always curious, always learning, and consistently willing to reinvent itself to meet the demands of its context.

=== Conclusion: A Journey of Balanced Success

Embarking on the entrepreneurial journey with the teachings of the Buddha may seem like an unconventional approach. Yet, if you observe closely, you'll realize that many success stories have emerged from this unique blend of spiritual wisdom and business acumen. Firms that operate on the Middle Path are not just more ethical, sustainable, and favored by consumers, they are also remarkably resilient—capable of transforming challenges into opportunities.

Thus, the Middle Path does not denote a compromise on success or dialing back on ambition. Instead, it redefines success, reaching beyond mere monetary gains to create a holistic success that celebrates profits, and dives deeper to find a purpose in contribution, adding value to the world we inhabit.

Walking the Middle Path in entrepreneurship means fostering a profitable business that is conscious of its socio-economic footprint, committed to a purpose beyond itself, and caters to its stakeholders with empathy and fairness. It's about grounding ambition with wisdom, and success with humility. This, perhaps, is the most enlightened form of entrepreneurship. As we journey down this path, we explore not just the landscapes of business, but also traverse the beautiful, often complex, terrains of our own selves.

Being an entrepreneur then becomes not just about leading a successful business; it's about leading a fulfilling life. And that

maybe, is the true
meaning   of
Entrepreneurial
Enlightenment.

== Entrepreneurial
Nirvana:
Achieving
Sustainable
Success and Inner
Peace   The
intricacies   of
entrepreneurship
are challenging to
navigate even with
traditional
business   acumen.
However,   by
drawing   upon
enduring wisdom
from   Buddha's
teachings, we can
harness   inner
peace   and
resilience   to
achieve
sustainable
success.   This
chapter   will
uncover how to
apply   these
principles to your
entrepreneurial
journey.

===   The

Intersection of Spirituality and Business

Rooted in ancient wisdom and inspired by modern business, "Entrepreneurial Nirvana" is a philosophy that emphasizes interconnectednes s, balance, and compassion in entrepreneurial pursuits. This philosophy promotes an integrated approach to entrepreneurship, viewing success not just in terms of financial gain, but also in attaining inner peace and personal fulfilment.

=== Foundational Principles of Buddha's Teachings

In striving for

Entrepreneurial Nirvana, it is essential to comprehend the core ideas of Buddha's teachings. Emphasizing mindfulness, compassion, and balance, these teachings encourage practitioners to reflect on their actions and their consequences, nurturing an expansive perspective beyond mere profit.

1. *The Four Noble Truths*: These focus on the reality of suffering, its causes (tanha, or desire), the possibility of overcoming suffering (nibbana or nirvana), and the eightfold

path that leads to its ending.

2. *The Eightfold Path*: This path serves as a guide to ethical conduct, mental discipline, and wisdom, including right understanding, right intention, right speech, right action, right livelihood, right effort, right mindfulness, and right concentration.

Applying these teachings into the realm of entrepreneurship does not mean turning your business into a religious project. Instead, it requires understanding these principles as frameworks for ethical, balanced, and insightful business practices.

=== Embracing Mindfulness in Business Decisions

In its essence, mindfulness is about staying present and aware in each moment. In the business context, mindful entrepreneurs consciously evaluate business decisions, considering their long-term repercussions on all stakeholders, including employees, customers, society, and the environment.

1. *Mindful Decision-Making*: This practice involves being fully present during the

decision-making process, observing your reactions and emotions, considering the broader implications of the decision, and approaching the process with a sense of calm and focus.

2. *Emotional Intelligence*: Mindful entrepreneurs understand and respect their own emotions and those of others, leading actions that resonate with empathy, mutual respect, and understanding.

Just as a tranquil pond accurately reflects the sky, a

mind unclouded by distraction or emotional turbulence can make wise and compassionate decisions.

=== Building Resilience through Inner Peace

Buddha's teachings stress the importance of mental discipline and inner peace. Resilience is required to confront the inevitable hurdles along the entrepreneurial path. Cultivating an inner sanctuary of peace allows for the development of this resilience.

1. *Meditation*: As a means to train your mind, regular meditation strengthens emotional

regulation, enhances creativity and problem-solving abilities, and bolsters resilience.

2. *Self-Compassion*: Kindness towards oneself during challenging times reinforces mental and emotional resilience, reminding you that setbacks are not failures but opportunities to grow and learn.

=== Ethical Entrepreneurship and Right Livelihood

Right Livelihood, an element of the Eightfold Path,

advocates for a vocation that neither harms nor exploits others. This high ethical standard, when applied in business, fosters goodwill and ensures a sustainable and resilient enterprise.

1. *Ethical Business Practices*: This involves creating fair policies for stakeholders, being transparent in operations, and making a conscious effort to reduce harm and enhance positive influence on the community and environment.

2. *Social*

Entrepreneurship: Businesses can embody Right Livelihood by tackling social issues and creating solutions that benefit both the enterprise and society.

=== Achieving Balance

Striking a balance between personal life and work is vital for overall well-being. Buddha's teachings encourage moderation in all spheres of life. By applying this concept in entrepreneurship, you can maintain equilibrium, reducing burnout and enhancing sustainable success.

1. *Work-Life Balance*: This involves setting boundaries to ensure personal time, promoting a healthy work environment, and prioritizing mental and physical health along with business growth.

2. *Balanced Stakeholder Engagement*: Nurturing a balanced approach towards all stakeholders ensures that no single entity is overloaded or overlooked, fostering a harmonious entrepreneurial ecosystem.

=== Bringing

Compassion into Leadership

Leadership in Entrepreneurial Nirvana centers on compassion and understanding. Buddha's teachings emphasize the importance of empathy in our interactions, a mindset that fosters strong, authentic relationships.

1. *Compassionate Leadership*: Leaders who practice kindness and understanding foster trust, enhance team morale, and stimulate an environment where creativity and productivity thrive.

2. *Impactful Communication*: Open lines of communication, actively listening, and speaking mindfully strengthen relationships and cultivate a supportive business environment.

Your path to Entrepreneurial Nirvana intertwines spirituality and business, forming an elevated understanding of entrepreneurial success—one that not only impacts your bottom line but also contributes positively to your personal growth, mental health and the world around you. By practicing mindful decision-making, resilient composure, ethical entrepreneurship, balanced living, and compassionate leadership, we align ourselves with the essence of Buddha's teachings, transforming our businesses and ourselves in the pursuit of entrepreneurial enlightenment.

www.ingramcontent.com/pod-product-compliance
Lightning Source LLC
Chambersburg PA
CBHW071100260726
48661CB00006B/2374